Jon Bon Jovi → Destination A

Wise Publications
London / New York / Sydney / Paris / Copenhagen / Madrid

Exclusive Distributors:
Music Sales Limited
8/9 Frith Street, London W1V 5TZ, England.
Music Sales Pty Limited
120 Rothschild Avenue, Rosebery, NSW 2018,
Australia.

Order No. AM950081
ISBN 0-7119-7004-1

Visit the Internet Music Shop at
http://www.musicsales.co.uk

Music arranged by Roger Day.
Music processed by Paul Ewers Music Design.

Printed in Great Britain by
Printwise (Haverhill) Ltd, Haverhill, Suffolk

Your Guarantee of Quality:
As publishers, we strive to produce
every book to the highest commercial standards.
The music has been freshly engraved and,
whilst endeavouring to retain the original running
order of the recorded album, the book has been
carefully designed to minimise awkward page
turns and to make playing from it a real pleasure.
Particular care has been given to specifying
acid-free, neutral-sized paper made from pulps
which have not been elemental chlorine bleached.
This pulp is from farmed sustainable
forests and was produced with special regard
for the environment.
Throughout, the printing and binding
have been planned to ensure a sturdy, attractive
publication which should give years of enjoyment.
If your copy fails to meet our high standards,
please inform us and we will gladly replace it.

Music Sales' complete catalogue
describes thousands of titles and is available
in full colour sections by subject, direct from
Music Sales Limited.
Please state your areas of interest and send
a cheque/postal order for £1.50 for postage to:
Music Sales Limited, Newmarket Road,
Bury St. Edmunds, Suffolk IP33 3YB.

1	Queen Of New Orleans	Page 4

2	Janie, Don't Take Your Love To Town	Page 10

3	Midnight In Chelsea	Page 16

4	Ugly	Page 22

5	Staring At Your Window With A Suitcase In My Hand	Page 26

6	Every Word Was A Piece Of My Heart	Page 33

7	It's Just Me	Page 40

8	Destination Anywhere	Page 49

9	Learning How To Fall	Page 54

10	Naked	Page 59

11	Little City	Page 64

12	August 7, 4:15	Page 70

13	Cold Hard Heart	Page 76

Queen Of New Orleans

Words & Music by
Jon Bon Jovi &
Dave Stewart

ba- by our love's just like your songs, the best ain't bad but the words are all wrong. It's time to

pack my bags,— it's time to just move on, she sang "John - nie I'm gone, I'm— gone,"–

and she was gone.

Me and Leigh-met sum-mer nine - ty five,— in a bur-gun-dy dress, look-ing fin - er than a French wine.
Made a move, man I felt hard when I put my hands in her cook-ie jar, she— was

danc-ing in the streets of New Or - leans. Ooh,—— danc-ing cheek to cheek in New Or -

- leans. Ooh,—— it was al-most like a dream.——

That night I

2

Janie, Don't Take Your Love To Town

Words & Music by
Jon Bon Jovi

Sit-ting here while you're fast a-sleep,— in the bath-room by— the sink,— tryin' to write the right— words

down. I turn out the lights,— close my eyes, there ain't no prayers or kiss good-night, what I'll for-

get to say— to-mor-row I'll— say now. Ja - nie, don't you take your love—

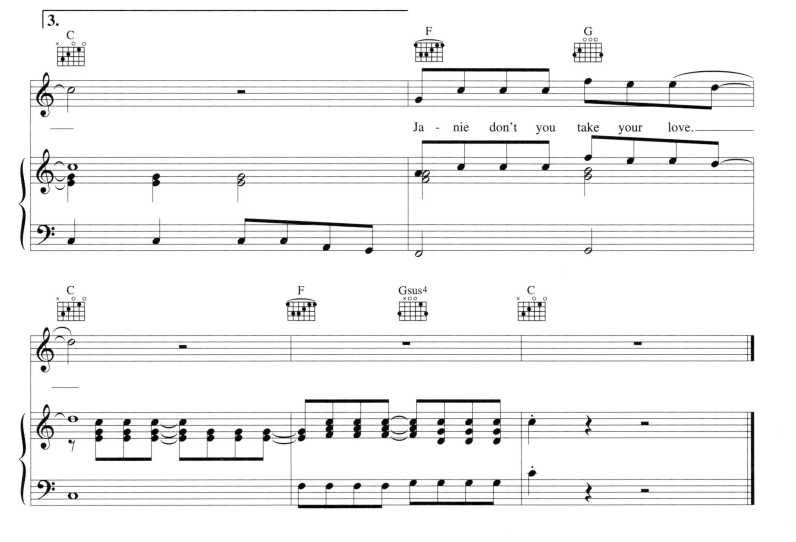

Ja - nie don't you take your love.

Verse 2:
I remember how it used to be
I was you and you were me
We were more than just the same
Now these shoes don't fit, my skin's too tight
When you want a kiss, I take a bite,
Let your heart call up the cops, read me my rights.

Last night I drank enough to drown
Raise a toast to your good looks and to my health
Look, we both know how much I've let you down
Janie, don't you take your love to town

Verse 3:
You deserve a shooter, a saint
Someone to give it to you straight
To find the soul through flesh and bone
My life's a treasure, full of sunny weather
But it's left me feeling cold
Now all you want to do is take me home.

I hated you the night you said you loved me
I hated you 'cause I couldn't love myself
I'm begging you now baby please just hold me
I got one foot in and one foot off the ground.

3

Midnight In Chelsea

Words & Music by
Jon Bon Jovi &
Dave Stewart

se - ri - ous as heart at - tacks, it takes a lit - tle bit of get - tin' used to. The

old man with the whis - key stains,___ lost the night for-got his name, his poor wife will sleep a -

lone a - gain. And it ain't hard to un - der - stand___ why she's

hold - ing on to her own hand.___ It's mid - night in Chel -

-sea, midnight_____ in Chel - sea,
Sha la la la sha___ la la,___ sha la la___ la sha

1.
___ la la,___ no - one's ask - ing me ___ for fa - vours, no-one's
sha la la___ la no - one's sha

look - ing for___ a sa - viour, they're too bu - sy_____ sav - ing me.
___ la la,___ sha la la la sha___ la la. ___)

2.
no-one's pinned their dreams on me, no-one's ask - ing me to bleed, I'm the
___ la la. ___)

where young lov - ers kiss good - bye, I leave my soul and just move on, and wish that

I was there to sing this song.

- sea, mid - night in Chel - sea.
Sha la la la sha la la, sha la la la la

It's mid - night in Chel - No-one's ask-ing me for fa - vours, no-one's
la la, la la, sha la la la la

Verse 2:
I seen a lone Sloane Ranger drive
Seems her chauffeur took a dive
And sold her secrets to the Sun.
And later in a magazine
I finally figured what it means
To be a saint, not a queen.

Two lustful lovers catch a spark
And charged their shadows in the dark,
Someone's getting off tonight
Of a big red bus that's packed so tight
It disappears in a trail of light
Somewhere someone's dreaming baby
It's all right, it's midnight in Chelsea.

4   Ugly

Words & Music by
Jon Bon Jovi &
Eric Bazilian

1. If you're ug-ly, I'm ug-ly too, in your eyes the sky's a dif-ferent

(Verses 2 & 3 see block lyric)

ug - - - ly, yeah yeah yeah,____

yeah yeah yeah.____

Ug - ly, ug - ly, all of us____ just feel like that some days,____ ain't no

D.%. al Coda

{rain-bow in the sky,} *{cure that you can buy,}* when you feel U. G. L. Y. and that's ug - - - ly. So

⊕ Coda

you.

I wish I was— as beau-ti-ful as you.

rall.

Verse 2:
And I wish I was a camera sometimes
So I could take your picture with my mind
Put it in a frame for you to see
How beautiful you really are to me.

Verse 3:
So if you're ugly, I'm ugly too
If you're a nut then I must be a screw.
If you could see yourself the way I do
You'd wish you were as beautiful as you.

Staring At Your Window
With A Suitcase In My Hand

Words & Music by
Jon Bon Jovi

You think you know— me just be-cause— you know— my name—

you think you see me,— 'cause you've seen ev-'ry line on— my

face. You want to want— me, just be-cause— I say that I— want

you, but does it mat-ter,— if a-ny-thing— I'm say - ing is— the truth.—

You need some-bo-dy, some-bo-dy to hold— on to,—

you place your bets,____ 'cause no one thinks_ they'll lose.

2.

The light of love_ can blind you till you

cov - er up_ your eyes_ and you try to find_ the rea - son

not to say_ good - bye._ It's the curse of ev - 'ry sail - or

stand - ing on— dry land,— star - ing at— your win - dow with a

suit - case in my hand.

The night is fad - ing— like my old— tat - too,—

a heart and a dag - ger___ that says "For - ev - er."___

suit - case in my hand.

6 Every Word Was A Piece Of My Heart

Words & Music by
Jon Bon Jovi

love,   there's no   hate,   I   left   them   there   for   you—   to   take,—

— but   know   that   ev - 'ry   word—   was   a   piece   of   my   heart.—

1.
You've   been   the—   blood—

2, 𝄋.
Have   I—   said—

— too   much,—   may - be   I   have - n't   said—   e - nough,—

7

It's Just Me

Words & Music by
Jon Bon Jovi

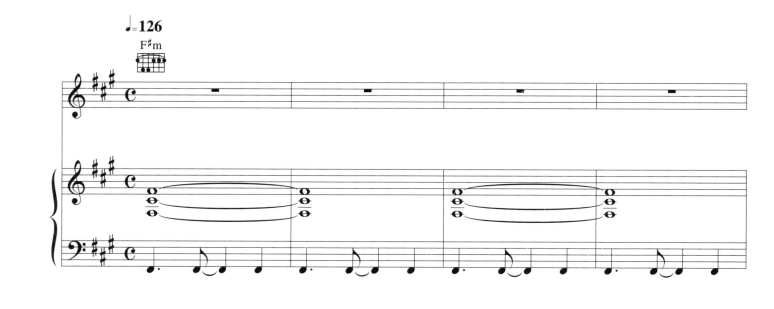

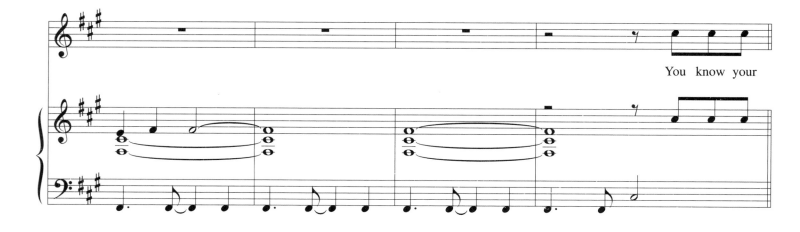

You know your

favour-ite old pair of shoes, the ones with the hole in the toe you won't

you bet - ter be - lieve

there's just one thing you need, oh can't

you see it's just me ba - by, it's just

me ba - by, if there's just one thing that you should keep

it's just me,   it's just   me,   (baby)

it's just me,   (baby.)

F♯m *(Solo ad lib.)*

A   E

Repeat ad lib. F♯m

8

Destination Anywhere

Words & Music by
Jon Bon Jovi

(1.) Hey babe it's
(2.) Ba - by we both been

me   parked out - side____   your house,___
run - ning up - hill for too long,   we both____

I know that he's a - sleep____ so lis - ten to me____ now.____
set - tled for some - thing, got noth - ing and we both know it's wrong.____

Dar - lin' I'm tired of liv - in' just in your dreams, I'm____
Go on ad - mit it, we lived it, I'm leav - ing get your boots and come

get - tin' out,____ you know we both____ sold our souls, we're
on, I've got my coat and my keys, I need

just grow - ing old in this sleep - y dead - end town.____
you next to me, then I'm gone.____ (Come on.)

50

Learning How To Fall

Words & Music by
Jon Bon Jovi

9

1. I was walk-ing on— a wire, look-ing down there was no

(Verses 2 & 3 see block lyric)

net, now I'm stand-ing at— your door,

me and my last ci - ga - rette. (Ah.)   (black.)

Now this cir - cus has left town,   this

clown has got— to get his feet back on the ground.— I'm learn - ing how— to fall,—

To next section

(down.)   I'm learn - ing how to fall,—

Verse 2:

Yeah we've been through this before
Too late to cover up my tracks
Damn the fool who begs for more
I'll take my past and paint it black.

Verse 3:

I was standing in the light
There were faces all around,
I put my gloves up for a fight
One sucker punch and I was down.

Naked

Words & Music by
Mark Hudson, Greg Wells
& Jon Bon Jovi

My friend had a girl-friend, she liked her drink,— sucked the head off her la-ger, threw me a wink,— and she said to— me— "Bud-dy what's your sign?"

Little City

Words & Music by
Jon Bon Jovi

1. I got my call light on, gim - me
(Verses 2 & 3 see block lyric)

one more fare to-night,_____ just get me

To Coda ⊕

ov - er the bridge,__ I can see_____ those shin - y bay lights._____

You know I'm nev - er a - lone__ but I'm feel-ing lone-ly to - night,__

whisper: (Damn!) I got my last cig - ar - ette but I

la la la, sha la la la la la,

sha la la la la la oh.

God let these wheels roll to where the girls are pret-ty, where the

nights ex-plode and life is still liv-ing down this op-en road, the

arms of pi - ty wait to greet me to - night___ in lit - tle ci - ty.

Coda

Repeat to fade

Verse 2:
In my rear view mirror
I see someone else's hairline
I hear that fire in your eyes
Is on the rock and doing hard time.
And the grapes of wrath, they're on the vine
There's wine in this dirt
Here love ain't love
It's just another four letter word.

Verse 3:
Now that cold gray fog's
Just a rolling down the highway
He's come to carry me home
It's put a little smile on my face.

12   August 7, 4:15

Words & Music by
Jon Bon Jovi

four — fif - teen. —

Verse 2:

The deputies went door to door
Through all the neighbourhood
They said, I got some news to tell you folks
I'm afraid it ain't so good.
Somehow something happened
Someone got away
Someone got the answers
For what happened here today.

Verse 3:

Now the people from the papers
And the local TV news
Tried to find the reason,
Cop dogs sniffed around for clues.
Someone shouted "Hit and run"
The coroner cried "Foul"
Her blue dress was what she wore
The day they laid her body down.

Verse 4:

I know tonight that there's an angel
Up on Heaven's highest hill
And no one there can hurt you baby
No one ever will.
Somewhere someone's conscience
Is like a burning bed
The flames are all around you
How you gonna sleep again?

13 Cold Hard Heart

Words & Music by
Jon Bon Jovi

You said you loved— to watch— me sleep,

you put your head— down on— my— chest, to hear me breathe.

D.%. al Coda

you're the one___ to run___ babe, then you don't feel___ the hurt.___

Coda

heart. what's it gon - na take?

Verse 2:
I was a lover lost at sea
You found me washed up on the beach
You took me home, you gave me breakfast
I said I'd offer you protection but you didn't charge a fee.

Verse 3:
Her hair so brown and eyes so green
You used to say I made good company
She'd bring me wine and sip her tea
Then you'd give yourself what you could give to me.